Recent decades have provided Christians with an increasing interaction with various world religions. The growth of immigration from non-Christian nations combined with a greater global awareness through travel and communication have confronted Diaspora Christians with the reality of diversity in faith, culture and practices. This book which is in your hand will remind you that many men and women in the Bible served God even more tremendously in a foreign land than in their own home country. Reading this book will help Diaspora Christians to mobilize their minds and hearts to see the evangelistic purpose of God for them and their church in whatever country they are in. But this book is not only for Diaspora churches. It is also for "Welcomer" churches, since it will help them to understand how to integrate with the Diaspora churches, to cooperate and recognize their common ground of mission with the intention of reaching the lost together.

Pastor Daniel Habte
Eritrean Church Planter
Amarillo, Texas

This is a great piece of work that must be made available for Africans to read. Abeneazer has carefully outlined our challenges we face or mistakes we do as African Christians.

Owusu Ansah Boakye
Ghanaian PhD Candidate, Texas State University

This profound and critical small book is a wake-up call for today's church to let go of its cultural stereotypes and instead develop a kingdom mindset to proclaim the Gospel in this globalized world. Abeneazer points out some of the main reasons why churches, particularly in the African Diaspora, are not cross-culturally evangelistic. His strong Biblical and experiential reflections exhibit his deep desire to draw us all towards God's heart of seeking the lost. His work advised and challenged me as I am in the process of getting out of my Ethiopian comfort zone to reach out to other cultures. It led me to repent of my ignorance, corrected my inclination toward "Missiopessimism" and helped to equip me for further kingdom work. For anyone concerned with Christian mission, I believe that this book is worth reading.

Mehari Tedla
Ethiopian MA student, Columbia International University;
Former South-West EvaSUE Regional Coordinator

This book is an important contribution to the Diaspora Church which represents a massive amount of observation and careful thinking. Abeneazer inspires and re-energizes the Diaspora Church Christians to share the Gospel with others with love and passion regardless of the challenges facing the Church today. As a Diaspora Christian in Europe, I have found the book to be eye-opening and it gives me a fresh perspective on the greatest mission of all.

Engineer Mintesinot T. Wodajo
Sweden

This book helps us to see the Gospel as the solution for the needs and challenges of the African Diaspora. Having lived in both Africa and America, in both lack and abundance, I have seen that material things have never changed a person's life for eternity. Only the Gospel does. The legacy that we want to pass on to future African descendants is a life transformation which comes from fully embracing the Gospel of Jesus Christ.

Emmanuel Ambane
Cameroonian minister among International Students; Old Dominion University, Virginia Beach, VA

Abeneazer has done it – he has enlightened us on how to bear much fruit in the West as Diaspora cross-cultural evangelists. This is a book that will challenge, encourage and move us forward with an agenda that is God-centered and Christ-exalting and driven by the Holy Spirit.

Kennedy Mulinge
Kenyan Assistant Director
South Carolina Christian Chamber of Commerce

It is a book that should be read by everyone who profess Jesus Christ as his Savior and Lord, since every believer in the Son of God is a "Diaspora" for he is living in the earthly world, longing for a better country- the heavenly one. For those who are planning to get engaged in cross cultural mission work, it is all the more a "must read" one.

Blene Moltotal
Former Chairwoman of EvaSUE Board

A Reflection on Diaspora Cross-Cultural Evangelism: An African Perspective

A Reflection on Diaspora
Cross-Cultural Evangelism:
An African Perspective

Abeneazer Gezahegn Urga

Foreword by Dr. Christopher R. Little

Table of Contents

Foreword 1

Acknowledgements 3

Preface 5

1 Disunity: A Distraction for Cross-Cultural
Evangelism... 7

2 Language Acquisition: A Door for Cross-
Cultural Evangelism 11

3 The Jonah Syndrome: The Archaic Disease in
the Current World 17

4 Missiopessimism: Lack of Faith and Joy on the
Frontlines... 21

5 Church Planting orChurch Splitting? That is
the Question! 27

6 "We Have No Silver and Gold but We Have the
Gospel": Preaching Vs. Social Work... 31

7 Obstacles for Diaspora Cross-Cultural Evangelists 39

8 Critical Engagement in Diaspora Cross-Cultural Evangelism.. 47

9 Ethnocentrism: the Universal Plague in the Diaspora.. 51

10 A Biblical Paradigm for the Diaspora Community 61

Study Questions for Group Discussions....69

Foreword

Books on the topic of mission have now become popular. Yet many of them are repeating what has already gone before. This book in your hands, however, is different. It makes a unique contribution by addressing a critical need for the global church at the beginning of the 21st century. In fact, it has been written for such a time as this.

First of all, it is penned by a well-informed African theologian and leader. The time for Africans to approach Scripture through a foreign lens, either Western or Asian, is long gone. African believers are now producing their own works for the benefit and blessing of their own communities as well as the global church. Although the author is keenly aware of historical and cultural issues outside his own context, he interacts with the Bible from his Ethiopian background. He offers vital insights to his own ethnic community and to all others willing to join in the conversation. For this reason alone, the book merits attention.

It also contributes to a fast growing area of research related to Diaspora missiology. There are approximately 600 diasporic communities in the Western hemisphere and the number is growing annually. As many of these communities either carry the Christian faith with them or are incorporated into the church after arriving, they are now confronted with the call to reach their neighbors with the Gospel. Yet, as the author observes, these communities have all too often become insular, indifferent, and even confused, regarding their relationship to the Great Commission. They face a new reality far from their countries of origin and are wondering how to not only survive but thrive.

This is why this book is so needed, so significant. It uncovers this predicament and winsomely engages it. In short, it challenges Diaspora churches to move outward, forward, and upward, to nothing less than discipling secular, postmodern Western nations for Christ. It is filled with perceptive insights, pertinent suggestions, and practical steps to apply in response to God's missionary call upon their communities. Just like the Gentile church desired to return the debt to the Jerusalem church for having received the Gospel from it (Rom. 15:27), our non-Western brothers and sisters who now live in lands from which their missionary ancestors hail, can embrace the joyous privilege of befriending and witnessing to their descendants in the power of the Holy Spirit.

In the end, the book attempts to awaken a sleeping giant. Diasporic communities have not arrived in the West by chance or coincidence. At a time when Western Christianity is in decline, they have arrived in the perfect timing and will of God not ultimately for their own sakes but for the sake of the nations. Only heaven knows what would happen if the growing diasporic community in the West would rise to the challenge that stands before them. May God be pleased to use this book to awake this giant!

Christopher R. Little, PhD
Professor of Intercultural Studies
Columbia International University
January 2015

Acknowledgements

I would like to express my greatest appreciation to those who assisted my wife and me in our cross-cultural ministry. I am so grateful for our co-laborers in ministry throughout the world and want to thank them for their partnership in the Gospel.

I am so grateful for the Root Cellar ministry of Portland who has been serving the Diaspora from all over the world by being devoted to meeting the needs of foreigners and strangers in their land. Thanks for giving us opportunities to serve alongside you.

I appreciate Grace Church of Columbia for allowing us to worship and serve with you for three wonderful years. Thanks for your patience as I was learning how to minister cross-culturally in your midst.

Thank God for Clemson Presbyterian Church, for you have been our partners in every way even before my arrival in the United States as my wife's fiancé and as an international student. More specifically I would like to thank Reverend Rick Brawner and his ministry – Reformed University Fellowship International – for taking us on board and allowing us to be messengers of the Gospel among the international students.

I am so grateful for the International Student Association of Columbia International University (Dr. Mull, Dean Swift, Ronny, Priscilla, Lillian and Angela). It was a blessing and a joy to serve with you and among you. I have learned a lot and was blessed by you. I have been blessed to get to know most of you in the International Students' Prayer Group. How great it was to hear your stories and prayers in many languages. Miss you all. May God bless all the faculty of CIU seminary that invested in me in many respects. Thank you to The Hub 2013/14 team (Dr. Barnett, Dr. Smither, Jamie, Landon and

Rachel) as well. It was fun serving the "Missionary God" in the mission of God with you.

How can I forget the kindness of the First Baptist Church of Portland: its pastoral/administrative staff and its members? I praise God for your invaluable support and friendship as we ministered together in Portland. Thank you Pastor Melese W/Tsadik, the Koltys and the Rickeys for your frequent encouraging phone calls. It meant a lot to me during my frontline ministry period.

Thank you to the Almquists for your hospitality and the Ethio-Eritrean Fellowship of Westbrook, Maine, for your acceptance of me as a minister of God without any reservation. You all stood by my family and me in times of need. Thanks for your prayers and encouragement. Thanks Abdi Duale and his faith-filled wife for their partnership in ministry. Thanks for allowing me to be part of your invaluable contribution to fulfillment of the Great Commission.

My wife has been a constant support in my ministry. Thanks for believing in me. I am blessed to have you. Dave Kimball and his mom have been helpful and kind to us. We appreciate your flexibility! Lebeza Alemu, a modern day Gaius, thanks for your love and hospitality. I am glad that the powerful Gospel is depicted in your ministry. You show the inseparability of Gospel witness and displaying the love of Christ in action. Girum Behailu, thanks for your kind encouragement and partnership in the work of the Gospel. Thanks to East Park Printing for your kindness and help.

Many thanks to Cindy Udall, Nahom Tegene, Mehari Tedla, Dr. Chris Little, Mintesnot Temesgen, Emmanuel Ambane, Owusu Ansah Boakye, Pastor Daniel Habte and Blene Moltotal for your critique of the manuscript. I have learned many things from all of you and God has enriched my cross-cultural ministry through and because of you. May God be glorified because of his marvelous works through us all.

Preface

This book has three major components: First, it is a reflection. It is what I have been pondering and praying about and also preaching and teaching as I was doing cross-cultural evangelism as a Diaspora among Americans, people from Africa and people groups from other regions. This is somewhat a journal of my journey, just made a bit more structured and presentable. Thus, in writing this book I was "building the plane while flying it."

Second, this book is an exploration of the experiences and potential of Diaspora people groups, specifically Africans in the United States. "Diaspora" here is used for individuals as well as groups who are here in the United States as international students, refugees, immigrants and also missionaries sent to the United States from other countries. It designates people who live outside of their homeland.

Third, this book is about the importance of cross-cultural evangelism as opposed to evangelism exclusively within one's own people group. It is about going the extra mile to convey the message of the Gospel while crossing language and cultural barriers. It is about reaching out to people who are different than us.

In these pages I have attempted to explore and focus on the more general or common issues facing Diaspora believers rather than discussing exceptional breakthroughs or successes. I have attempted to at least mention instances of positive progress, but I have spent the majority of my time discussing hurdles to be overcome in hopes that the cross-cultural ministry of the Diaspora can be maximized. Thus it is my sincere hope that God will use this small book in your hands to inspire you in your life and ministry as you strive to make the Mighty God known among the nations in the Diaspora.

1
Disunity:
A Distraction for Cross-Cultural Evangelism

I just hung up the phone before starting to write this. I was driven to prayer because of the conversation, and the time of prayer produced the following thoughts. I was astounded and became indignant at the same time when I realized afresh – through the phone conversation – how the enemy is deterring the Church, especially the Diaspora Church, from doing her job of sharing the Gospel of Jesus Christ to the nations.

Disunity in the Church existed even in the time of Jesus (among the twelve apostles) and Paul (in the early Church). Jesus had to remind the apostles repeatedly that they should not fight with each other. Rather, they should forgive and be servants of one another. Before he went to the cross, Jesus prayed for unity among his followers so that the watching world would know the love of the sending Father and of Jesus himself (John 17:1-26). Paul addressed disunity within the church in nearly all of his epistles. Some of the churches he wrote to experienced disunity because of differences in leadership and gifting, others because of ethnic differences: Jews vs. Gentiles. Paul had to remind some believers that "we are one body" (Rom. 12:5), "that there be no division among you, but that you be united in the same mind and the same judgment" (1 Cor. 1:10), that "dissensions [and] divisions" are the works of the flesh (Gal. 5:20), that the unity of God and humanity gave a presupposition for the unity of Jews and Gentiles in Christ (Eph. 2:11-22). As a result, believers are to be "eager to maintain the unity of the Spirit in the bond of peace" (Eph. 4:3), that believers in the community should strive to maintain unity so as to create a conducive environment for solidarity (Eph. 5:21-6:9; Col. 3:18-4:1; Philemon 8-22), and that those in conflict should agree with each other (Phil. 4:2).

Unity is also emphasized in other parts of Scripture: James reprimanded those who show partiality (Jas. 2:1-7); he also points out that fleshly desires breed discord among believers (Jas. 4:1). Both Peter and Paul encourage husbands and wives to be unified and treat each other properly to bring about order; John the elder reminds his readers that a person's unity and oneness with his or her brothers signifies his or her unity with God through Christ, because love for a brother indicates love for God. Again, John, the beloved disciple, declares that redeemed people "from every tribe, and language and people and nation" will sing in unison for the slain Lamb of God before the throne of God (Rev. 5:9).

The motif of unity is found throughout the New Testament, but why is it so important? I believe, first of all, unity is not just an end; it is a means to an end. Believers' unity, in spite of ethnicity, socio-economic background and other differences, attracts people to God. It points out that the message of the Gospel and salvation blessings are not confined to one people group. Thus it calls people from where they are and welcomes people to come in to the diverse family of God. Unity is the reflection of love in spite of significant diversity and plurality.

Secondly, unity is not just a means; it is also an end. This unity should be seen as two-fold. The unity of believers, as John states it in his epistle, automatically indicates their unity with God. Sin disunited, divided and separated humanity from God. But through and in Christ, believers are able to be reunited, reunified and rejoined together with God. This vertical aspect of salvation blessings has a directly proportional effect horizontally – a man-to-man effect. Unity with God dissolves disunity with each other. Unity with God leads to unity with one another. It dispels disunity, discord and separation from each other (Col. 3:11; Eph. 2:11-22).

The Diaspora Church is being rocked by personal, ethnic, political, and language divisions. Pride, selfish ambition and competitiveness have crept in and have distracted believers from becoming one in heart and mind. This in turn has affected the furtherance of the Gospel among the unreached people groups who are literally next door and across the street.[1]

Anger, disagreements, serious conflicts and court cases are taking up the time of the Diaspora Church (and the church in general). Satan – God's archenemy – is benefitting and rejoicing. The Diaspora Church needs to be an instrument of God instead of being a handy instrument of the flesh, the world and the devil. Solidarity as a result of the finished work of Christ should be the hallmark of the Diaspora Church.

Some unbelievers have distanced themselves from Diaspora believers who are from their same country because of the failure of the Diaspora Church to become unified in diversity. Others have insulted the name of God because of such divisions. Brothers and sisters, can we become representatives of Christ instead of repellents of unbelievers? When we have disagreements, can we apply the principles of Matthew 18:15-35 instead of the principles of 1 Corinthians 6:1-8, handling conflict in a godly way?

---

[1] For instance, this is an issue among Ethiopians in the Diaspora, see "The East African Church in New England" published by Emmanuel Gospel Center, (accessed February 14, 2015),
https://sites.google.com/a/egc.org/newenglandsbookofacts/new-england-s-book-of-acts/section-two-group-reports/the-east-african-church-in-new-england#EE.

2
Language Acquisition:
A Door for Cross-Cultural Evangelism

Language (verbal or nonverbal) is a primary communication tool between God and man, and between men themselves. It is a vehicle to understand and be understood by others. It is a means to express our satisfaction, frustration, experiences, thoughts and feelings. It is through the mediation of language that we have been able to understand the will and plan of God. It is through the instrument of language that Shakespeare and Chinua Achebe spoke to us using their literary works. Emperor Menilik II mobilized the Ethiopians against the Italians, Adolph Hitler convinced his followers to massacre the Jews and Barack Obama persuaded Americans to vote for him using language (but please do not miss the sovereignty of God in the background of all these events). The significance of language can be illustrated from four areas of Scripture.

The people of Babel were able to build the enormous tower because they were able to understand each other since everyone was speaking the same language. But they failed to understand each other, for their language was confused by the Lord. So, work ceased and they were dispersed (Gen. 11:1-9). In the book of Esther, we see that the Jews were saved from Haman's genocidal intent because a reversing letter was written to various people groups in "127 provinces, to each province in its own script and to each people in its own language, and also to the Jews in their script and their language" (Esther 8:9). The same message was sent in various tongues because the message was essential. It was a matter of life and death.

By the same token, in the book of Acts, the disciples had to speak in tongues of each person that came from various nations to celebrate Pentecost so that they could grasp "the mighty works of God" (Acts 2:1-11). Paul, who was multilingual, also asks: "For 'everyone who calls on the name of the Lord will be saved.' How then will they call on him in whom they have not believed? And how are they to believe in him of whom they have never **heard**? And how are they to **hear** without someone preaching? And how are they to preach unless they are sent?" (Rom. 10:13-15a). People have to hear in a language they can comprehend so that they can call upon Jesus and be saved. Time and again, language is critical in mission, especially cross-cultural mission.

Language is an essential channel in the Diaspora missionary work. People come from all sorts of backgrounds: various continents, hundreds of countries, thousands of tribes, cultures, experiences, etc. The variety of cultures increases the complexity of the relationships among individuals and groups of people. Thus a Diaspora missionary has to know the language of the people they are trying to reach, since this will help them grasp the culture, experiences and expectations of those people. It will also help them to express their own needs, opinions, identity and expectations in their relationships with the people.

The Diaspora community is incredibly complex. These people come from various tongues, peoples, and nations. Some have gone through traumatic situations like rape, imprisonment, refugee camps, severe poverty, wars, genocides, etc. Some come from educated, peaceful, and calm areas. They are here – legally or illegally – to improve their situation through education or employment, pursue the American dream or escape a predicament in their homelands. Some are Muslims (from nominal to fanatical), others Christians (from all sorts of denominations), yet others have acclimated to their current home and embraced the postmodern, relativistic kind of ideology and lifestyle.

Some speak Somali, some French, some Amharic, or Oromifa or Tigringa, or British English, or Arabic or Portuguese. You can also add Swahili, Kirundi, Kikongo, Dinka or Lingala. How do we communicate with each other? How can you express some simple ideas like "Where is the bus station?" or "Why and when did you come here?" let alone explaining deep theological and spiritual concepts like sin, salvation, and the Trinity to the guy next door who has no idea about your language? As a Diaspora minister, I have struggled in communicating the Gospel to Diasporas from other cultures. I was able to use English to convey the Gospel to Somalis, Eritreans, Sudanese, and Burundese. But when I encounter a person who only speaks Arabic or French, the communication barrier is in place preventing me from speaking about Jesus.

So what should happen? Recently, I asked my French-speaking Christian friend why he is not trying to reach his Somali friends. I told him that he could study Somali or Arabic or improve his English since he was going to stay here where this people group is. He answered me simply: "It is difficult." My friend was right – language study *is* difficult. It is not an easy task. Language study requires repetition, patience, hard work, prayer, small baby steps and progressing "two steps forward and one step back." But compared to the lostness of people, compared to the reality of hell, compared to the bliss of the Gospel, compared to the degrading but liberating cross of Christ, it is nothing. If I can compare it with the grueling labor of some of the Diaspora believers who strive to succeed in the pursuit of happiness or the American dream, cross-cultural ministry is simple, and language study is a piece of cake! Some Diaspora believers work 18-20 hours per day. They have no break. I understand that when one comes to the States or to Europe, the expectation and the burden from back home is unbearable. And I commend and respect those who work hard to break the cycle of poverty and to support families and friends who still reside in their native countries.

But my challenge to my hard-working – at times workaholic – believing Diaspora friends is this: can you also see the poverty of the souls around you? Can you have compassion on the lost next door or next to you at your work place? Can you also work hard to enable them to cross from death to life? Can you become intentional in engaging yourself in cross-cultural ministry? Can you also win souls, not just bread? In order to do this, you might have to buy a French or Somali dictionary. You might have to take an hour off from your shift and lose that $7.50 or $9.00 so that your unbelieving Somali friend could teach you his language and culture at Starbucks or Chick-fil-A.

Or it might mean not just hanging out with people who speak your language. I know some Ethiopians who have lived in the USA for decades but just speak Amharic or Oromifa or Tigrigna and have never learned English except very basic phrases, because they are swallowed by their own people group. They work at an Ethiopian- owned business, go to an Ethiopian church, hang out with Ethiopians on holidays, attend the funerals, weddings or birthdays of Ethiopians, and Facebook chat with Ethiopians about Ethiopia. This also applies to other Africans in the Diaspora, but I just want to show some typical examples from my own countrymen. This is a fatal mistake, especially for Christians who are commanded to make disciples of all nations. At least for the sake of their children who are growing up in the host culture, parents should become intentional and proactive in teaching themselves the mainstream language of their residential country, if not at all for the sake of the Gospel!

There are a number of churches, philanthropic organizations, and individuals who willingly offer host-culture language classes for free or for a low cost. This is especially true for English as a foreign language. The Diaspora Christians, especially Africans who tend to congregate themselves with their own language speakers, have no excuse for not learning a language in a time such as this if they have the opportunity. Nothing is out of reach. Nigerians, Ghanaians and some Kenyans and Ethiopians should be commended for their bold, intentional approach to Diaspora cross-cultural evangelistic work in the West. But by far, most Africans are shy, passive and unintentional in learning other languages and cultures, preferring to cling to their own. To sum up, notice that at the Second Advent, it is not just English or Amharic or French speakers who will appear before the throne. It is *"a great multitude that no one could number, from every nation, from all tribes and peoples and* **languages***, standing before the throne and before the Lamb, clothed in white robes, with palm branches in their hands, and crying out with a loud voice, 'Salvation belongs to our God who sits on the throne, and to the Lamb!'* (Rev. 7:9-10).

Therefore, let us engage ourselves in the Diaspora cross-cultural missionary work, having Revelation 7:9-10 as our missionary goal to be realized soon, for this is the goal of mission: worshiping the Lamb in all languages before the throne of God.

3
The Jonah Syndrome:
The Archaic Disease in the Current World

The eighth century BC prophet, Jonah, was a sick man. The syndrome he suffered is as old as sin. This syndrome has been an incessant problem of the church of Christ throughout its history. Even at the genesis of the New Testament era the apostles struggled with the same syndrome. This syndrome happens for several reasons: at times because of ethnocentrism, at other times because of bad theology, or indifference and ignorance. In later years, in the Reformation period for instance, the Protestant church suffered from the Jonah syndrome because of bad hermeneutics, which gave birth to bad theology that confined the work of mission to *the apostles alone.* What was the Jonah syndrome specifically? And how is this syndrome affecting the Diaspora church in completing its current task?

Jonah was sent by God to the Assyrian city of Nineveh to speak against its evil. But Jonah fled from this call and tried to go in the other direction, because he did not want the Ninevites to escape God's judgment. In other words, he knew God is merciful; thus, if these enemies of Israel repented, he knew they would be spared. So Jonah's solution was disobeying the Sender.

Jonah was a very nationalistic, ethnocentric prophet, who, as many Jews did, wanted to see God's wrath come down upon the enemies of the Hebrews. He wanted mercy to be denied to the evil Ninevites. In so doing, he committed several instances of theological suicide. He forgot that God is the God of the nations, not just of the

Hebrews. He forgot that God was present everywhere – even in Joppa, Tarshish and Nineveh. He forgot that he was a messenger, not a manager of God's mission. He forgot that the God of heaven and earth and the sea has a message for every tribe, tongue, nation and people. He forgot that God's message is twofold: mercy for those who sin and commit evil but repent and forsake their old ways and judgment for those who ignore his warning.

The Jonah syndrome can be seen among Christians in the act of hoarding a critical message from the lost – both near and far – because of indifference, ethnocentrism, ignorance, disobedience or a judgmental mindset toward those we don't like or who are different from us. For instance, many American evangelical churches suffer from this syndrome. Terrorism and other nationalistic movements against the West, specifically against the United States, have created a climate of fear, hatred, indifference and Jonah's judgmental mindset among too many American Christians. Fox News and CNN are too often the main source of this information for church members in understanding and dealing, for instance, with Muslims. As a result, there are few American workers among the Muslims next door or on Main Street. Hence, the Gospel message is hindered in its flow among peoples who badly need to hear it.

The Diaspora church – specifically Africans – have not escaped this syndrome either. Ask someone from any other nation in Africa about their feelings on Somalis: they tend to feel negatively towards them. Piracy, the way they talk, their insistence on keeping their culture intact wherever they go, and Al-Shabaab have made the Somalis an object of hatred, indifference, and judgment as well as a source of fear. But is this the attitude Christians should have? Are we not told to love our neighbors as we love ourselves? Are we not called to love even our enemies?

The Jonah syndrome throws all that "love your enemies" and "love your neighbor" truth out the window. When the contemporary Church falls prey to the Jonah syndrome, they defiantly say that they would rather die than see God show mercy to Muslims. They choose flight, fear and deaf ears—anything rather than making these people their friends and sharing the Good News with them. We choose to show frowns or sullen faces rather than expressing the joy of the Lord through smiling and shaking the hand of a Muslim vendor at the halal market. We choose suspicion over trusting the Lord for whatever might happen through a relationship with Ahmed or Fatuma. African Diaspora Christians need to read their Bible with a correct hermeneutic and develop a good theology that propagates the love of one's neighbor – a Muslim neighbor, yes a Somali neighbor. The Diaspora church should come out of this attitude of monopolizing God in one culture. These churches need to realize that God is bigger than their culture or country. He is the God of all cultures. As Paul reminds us, "he made from one man every nation of mankind to live on all the face of the earth" (Acts 17:26).

As we have seen earlier, it is because of the Jonah syndrome that the Diaspora church does not take the initiative to learn other languages so as to share the Gospel relevantly. The antidote to the Jonah syndrome is found in two Commandments:

*"Hear, O Israel: The L*ORD *our God, the L*ORD *is one. You shall love the L*ORD *your God with all your heart and with all your soul and with all your might"* (Deut. 6:4; cf. Mark 12:30).

"...you shall love your neighbor as yourself" (Lev. 19:18; cf. Mark 12:31; Jas. 2:8).

If the African Diaspora churches truly grasp the implications of these two Commandments, they will be motivated to learn the languages and the cultures of the unreached and unengaged people groups, befriend Muslims, "obey God instead of Fox News"[2] or CNN, and proclaim God's wrath against sin and the availability of grace for those who repent. This could lead to the repentance of today's Ninevites— the so-called "dangerous" people groups.

---

[2] Stated by an American director of a mission organization in a personal conversation regarding most North Americans' attitude towards Muslims.

4
Missiopessimism:
Lack of Faith and Joy
on the Frontlines

My wife and I just had dinner with a ministry contact of ours who has extensive experience in Gospel ministry among the unreached Diaspora. Because we were beginning in the same type of ministry, we wanted to hang out and be encouraged and learn from him. But, on the contrary, we found our conversation extremely discouraging. My missionary brother was rather a Missiopessimist. What do I mean by that? Missiopessimism is defined or characterized by statements like: "Whatever I do, these people won't change. So I will change my vision." "Why should I preach the Gospel to them? I see no results." "Brother, I am done with them. I have tried many things to bring the good news to them." "It takes decades to get a convert among them."

There is also another way one can detect the implicit Missiopessimism ingrained in missionaries and Christians in general, especially among Americans. When a Muslim embraces the Gospel and joins God's family, there is loud celebration, but when there is a convert who used to be a cultural Christian or secular person or a single mom who struggled with some sort of addiction or a 15-year-old high school teenager, the celebration is not nearly so boisterous.[3]

The problem with such an attitude implies a very serious theological presupposition: that some people are extremely difficult

---

[3] This was pointed out to me by a Korean missionary to the Southeast Asian Muslims.

for the powerful God and his Gospel to reach while others are "easy" for God. When we look at this implicit assumption, we find an explicit error. For example, St. Luke tells us three times, in case we have missed it, that there will be great "joy in heaven over one sinner who repents" (Luke 15:7; cf. 15:10, 32). Notice that the joy does not specify previous religion or some sort of social standing, but simply "a sinner," any sinner. That is a description for a Muslim, a secular American, a Hindu guru, a Buddhist monk, a Beninese animist, a cultural Catholic or a homeless person who does not know Christ.

Missiopessimism, unless treated early, can be a fatal disease for missionaries. How is it possible that a once faithful, hard-working and compassionate missionary could have turned into an apathetic, discouraged and discouraging man of God? In that conversation I was told by him, directly and indirectly, to stop my effort to reach one of the most unreached people groups in the world. I was rebuking the idea quietly in my mind as I talked to my brother, but I also gently challenged him out loud that we still have to continue preaching to this specific people group. Then I started to think what could be the reasons for Missiopessimism among missionaries? Here are what I see as some of the causes:

The first one is burnout! Burnout is when a person is exhausted physically, mentally, and spiritually and does not have anything left in him. This happens when he gives little attention to feeding himself on God's Word, praying constantly, being filled with the Holy Spirit as well as giving out more and more from his reservoir from the past, relying on resources from a time when he was more spiritually vital. He focuses all of his attention on people, activities and ministry. Thus the believer (missionary) starts to be angry, impatient, compulsive, depressed, easily discouraged and have frequent conflicts with other coworkers or people he is trying to reach. The ministry task becomes something that **has to** be done. The missionary ignores the guidance of the Spirit and depends on his routine and past experience. Quiet time, rest, and studying the Word become tough and the missionary tries to get out of his dismal state by doing something else, like watching TV, having more ministry activities, or falling into an addiction, etc. Prayer and studying become dry and seem unproductive and useless.

The second cause for Missiopessimism is excessive missionary triumphalism. Because of past success and experience the missionary tries to apply everything that he did and used to his or her current context, and when something does not work as planned or when the missionary faces new challenges, his excessive triumphalism is reversed to excessive discouragement. Such missionaries do not want to learn another level of ministry challenge and God's faithfulness through it. They just want the old tactics every day like a formula or a machine, forgetting that God works in various ways in various times in various contexts. But it is essential to insert a caveat here. Unflinching faith that asserts that God can do anything at any time in any context should be differentiated from excessive triumphalism. Faith says that no matter what, God will ultimately win. Excessive triumphalism is characterized and identified when it suddenly cools off and becomes frozen when it is hit by challenges and obstacles. But faith stands where it is regardless. This leads us to the third cause.

The third cause for Missiopessimism is a certain kind of faithlessness that theologians call "under-realized eschatology." This brand of faithlessness does not appear as such at first glance because it has some spiritual expressions clothing it to make it appear true. This state of mind or attitude says, "God knows," "God is sovereign," "It is God's decision," but then it tries to abdicate responsibility. Missionaries with such a frame of mind preach the

Gospel, but they do not believe, albeit implicitly and at times unknowingly, in the power of the Gospel. They just do their task but they lack faith that God can change the hearts of those who are hearing it. They recite the creed but they deny its practical implications. They approach Gospel ministry "with...doubting...like a wave of the sea that is driven and tossed by the wind....[They are] double-minded [men], unstable in [their] ways" (James 1:6, 8). Thus they see no fruit, no results. And with vocabulary that seems spiritual, they preach their "double-minded" theology and approach to those who are there to work among the harvest, thus disheartening them.

The fourth cause of Missiopessimism is fear of disappointment. This is closely related to the fourth cause which we just saw, but it has a specific issue with it. The third one, faithlessness, was simply lacking faith, but this one is more personal. My wife expresses it in this way:

> It seems easier not to hope than to hope and then be disappointed. This version of Missiopessimism is sometimes viewed as acceptable because it seems so virtuous. After all, we don't want God to look bad — we don't want his reputation to be tarnished by us saying He'll do something and then Him not doing it. We protect His reputation, so we think, by not having any expectations. The reality is, though, that we are trying to protect *our* reputation! That is the ulterior motive. Externally, we just blame it on protecting God's glory and fame. But God does not need to be babied in this way. He is perfectly capable of handling his own reputation and he is able to do beyond all we could ask or imagine, according to his power that is at work within us (Eph. 3:19-20). He says we will receive, find, and walk through an open door — but first we must have great expectations, daring in faith and hoping against hope enough to ask, seek, and knock (Matt. 7:7-11).

Last but not least, Satan's direct assault on the ministry of the Gospel is another cause for Missiopessimism. The devil does not like the Gospel to spread. Instead, he hates it. He prefers building projects, water drilling, free medication, etc. much better than the preaching of the Gospel, the proclamation of the Good News. *That* he detests. Thus he tries to discourage Gospel workers by displaying vividly where they lack and stumble. For example, he showed my missionary friend that a couple of men from a church became Muslims, and that none of the kids he shared the Gospel with became believers. Satan magnified that in his mind as though the whole church had embraced Islam! That discouragement led to frustration and then hatred – yes, hatred. My brother was showing hatred towards the people he had once tried to reach. His compassion was gone. He forgot he was sent as a sheep among wolves (Matt. 10:16). He did not remember that the world is the one who hates us and not vice versa. That is a reverse theology.

But this hatred also develops when we focus on loving the people we are trying to reach with the Gospel and then expecting the same response back from them. That is again taking our eyes off of the Lord. People cannot fulfill our ultimate quest for love. Besides, we cannot expect people without hope and without Christ to give us what they themselves do not have. We are able to love because we have been touched and changed by the Source of love, which is God. John reminds us that *"love is from God, and whoever loves has been born of God and knows God. Anyone who does not love does not know God, because God is love. In this the love of God was made manifest among us, that God sent his only Son into the world, so that we might live through him. In this is love, not that we have loved God but that he loved us and sent his Son to be the propitiation for our sins."* (1 John 4:7-10). Satan is preaching the reverse message, asserting that we should expect people without Christ to love us back in a Christ-like way and behave like Christians.

We need to remember that even when "[Jesus] was in the world, and the world was made through him, yet the world did not know him. He came to his own, and his own people did not receive him" (John 1:10-11). But they "crucified and killed" him (Acts 2:23). Satan assaults the missionary's proper understanding and expectations of Gospel ministry, and points out various insignificant things that dishearten the Gospel worker. The Gospel worker then in turn becomes an instrument of Satan to discourage others.

We have now seen the causes of Missiopessimism, but what shall be done? There are a few suggestions I want to make. Missionaries should always watch out for their spiritual health. Regular, daily Bible reading, studying, memorizing, ceaseless private or group prayers, physical rest and also attention to a nutritious diet are essentials. The missionary should never stop having faith in whatever circumstance he finds himself in, and his eyes should focus on Christ so that circumstances do not deter the Gospel work where the missionary is striving. The missionary should seek to glorify God, not himself. Most missionaries struggle to motivate their supporters to give; thus they always feel the need to come up with some numbers or breakthroughs. But it is vital to remember that God is the one who provides even when we do not see visible outcomes in our ministry. Put God's glory truly first; do not just use it as a veneer while deep down looking for our own glory and success story. The missionary must realize that Satan is real and still at work. Though some suggest that he is on sabbatical, Scripture and even our own experience testify otherwise. But we need to rebuke him and tell him, "Be gone, Satan!" (Matt. 4:10); "Get behind me, Satan!" (Mark. 8:33). We "[should] not be outwitted by Satan; [by becoming] ignorant of his designs" (2 Cor. 2:11).

5
Church Planting or Church Splitting? That is the Question!

Recently I finished reading a book in Amharic which is titled *The Waking Bell.*[4] It seems to have been written to a sleeping and slumbering church of Christ in Ethiopia regarding Muslim evangelism. The book covers a number of topics, especially dealing with current issues in Islam, the growth of Islam worldwide, and the Islamic movement's strategies to take over Southern and Eastern Africa. At the end of the book, the author suggests various ways to reach Muslims. One of his concluding suggestions was this: "Those of you who have real vision, instead of tearing the existing body like an amoeba, go and plant churches in Afar, Ethio-Somaliland, Bale, Arsi, and Silte, and God will be with you."[5] He was encouraging church splitters to become true church planters. Instead of starting a new church by "stealing sheep" from an already existing church, it would be commendable to go where Christ's name is not known and where a local believing body scarcely exists (Rom. 15:20-21).

Church splitting is not an uncommon practice among Christians throughout the world. In America, church splitting sometimes happens because of carpet color or music preferences, or lack of ventilation or AC within the building where believers assemble to worship. In Ethiopia, a minister or a novice preacher who does not like to be under someone else but who just wants to

---

[4] My translation of the title.
[5] My translation of the words of Yagebagnal Bemnet, *Yemankiya Dewl* (Np: np, Hamle 2004 E.C.), 79.

lead by himself might split the church. Others split churches fleeing from church discipline, thus creating churches founded upon pouting. The Diaspora church has not escaped this issue. There are more church splitters than church planters. This church splitting habit of Diaspora preachers is also affecting their reputation by making them an object of gossip because of their divisive actions. They have become like amoeba by tearing the body and forming a colony nearby.

There are several reasons for church splitting among Diaspora churches. But I will stick with the four major ones for the sake of time and space. The first reason church splitting is happening, especially among East Africans, is because those who lead a church, of any amount of people, can easily get a religious visa. It is easier and faster to settle oneself in such a way in the US.[6] So, one can dare to split a small church of 20 people into two with eloquent, persuasive speech and reasoning just to get a paper.

The second reason is lack of humility. Maybe a newly arrived immigrant has been pastoring and leading a church in his home country. Thus when he comes to the West he cannot stand to be led and to be under another's shepherding ministry. Instead of strengthening and supporting the existing leaders, he becomes a source of dissension and division. He makes his own team and gets supporters to flock behind him, and so church splitting becomes inevitable. At times, the new-coming minister might see factual errors and negative practices within the existing church, but instead of taking time and trying to correct the wrong and deal with the issue head on, he chooses an easier way out: starting another. But the irony is that later the church splitter often becomes a target

---

[6] This was pointed out to me by an evangelist in the continent of Africa who came to study for a few years in the US.

and a victim of another church splitter. What goes around often comes around.

The third one is ethnocentric division. Here I am not talking about starting new churches so as to minister to those who cannot comprehend another language other than their own. I am referring to an insidious dividing or splitting an existing church based on language, geography or ethnicity so as to become a leader of certain groups as an end in itself. Hence, even behind the ethnocentrism there is that ulterior motive that urges and hungers for position and prestige. Mind here that in many African churches becoming a pastor is a way to be served rather than to serve. It is a prestigious position many lust after which is contrary to the model Christ has lived out before our own eyes (Mark 10:35-45). It is surely a "noble" thing to desire to be a leader in the church (1 Tim. 3:1), but the problem I am pointing out here is self-centered ambition regarding leadership that results in division.

The fourth factor is the lack of initiative from existing church leaders by taking wisely and properly the new gifted evangelist, pastor, or prophet and putting him under their supervision. For fear of leadership challenge and subsequent usurpation, most pastors avoid or watch the newcomer suspiciously from a distance. But through prayer and discernment they can take the initiative in befriending, nurturing, and guiding these new leaders so that they could be mentored and used in accordance with the particular church's structure and their gifting. This would avoid potential animosity and dissensions within Diaspora churches.

These major causes of church splitting in the Diaspora play a significant role in deterring the Church from her job of multiplying by evangelizing and congregating new believers into the body. The new- coming preachers and pastors in the Diaspora churches should humble themselves by sitting under others and learning. When they get the opportunity, like Paul, they should strive to break new grounds instead of laying a foundation on existing places (Rom. 15:20-21). And God will bless that. Instead of becoming a cause for pain, anger, and dissensions, they should be blessings to the unreached and the lost nations around them.

6
"We Have No Silver and Gold but We Have the Gospel": Preaching Vs. Social Work

There is extensive literature out there regarding the topic of Prioritism versus Social Work, so this humble little essay is surely a drop in the ocean, for I am not going to cover all the facets of the debate that need detailed discussion. But as an Ethiopian, as an African minister, and above all as a Bible-believing Christian, I will try to address this issue from a biblical and regional as well as an experiential perspective, focusing on the cross-cultural evangelistic ministry of the Majority World Christian Diaspora in America.

As many voices have opined, there is a huge tendency in the West to dichotomize or compartmentalize. This tendency has affected our current topic in tremendous ways. In the West, Christian workers often pigeonhole themselves as Prioritists (preaching first/alone) or Holists (social work and then preaching/social work alone). But for an African, even for the early Church fathers, this dichotomy is surely an absurdity. How can one choose one over the other? They are inseparable! You always preach the Gospel – it is your obligation in light of the Great Commission – but at the same time you do not forget if your neighbor is in need. Putting one of these things above the other does not fit the African worldview, for Africans have a communal lifestyle. But when you come to the West, you might not even know who your neighbor is! You just say "hi" to him once in a while, maybe when he opens his front door and rushes to his car, since "time is money" here.

This Western battle of Prioritists and Holists has unfortunately made its way to Africa and other Majority World areas through uncontextualized, foreign worldview driven trainings. Not only the dichotomistic inclination of my brothers and sisters in the West, but also a postmodern society that highly emphasizes the equality of men as well as justice, autonomy and fairness has played an invaluable role in our current discussion. This generation – the postmodern generation – has become virtually connected to everyone from everywhere via the internet. This global exposure has made my generation become aware of widespread problems and fight for the rights of others, speak out on behalf of the oppressed, and attempt to achieve the freedom of the enslaved and ill-treated. This is highly commendable. Yet this global connectedness tends to magnify the physical sickness of the world (which surely does exist and should not be ignored by the church!) while not spending much time depicting the sickness of the world's souls and its spiritual ailments. I am afraid that this generation has missed a crucial point just like Johannes Hoekendijk, who missed the heart and the goal of mission when he played an instrumental role in the "de-sacralising of mission and [the] depreciation of the church as the agent of God's mission."[7] I am concerned that the misguided vision of the World Council of Churches that met in Uppsala, Sweden, in 1968 is being realized. I am afraid that **"The World Sets the Agenda"** for the church of Christ,[8] thus making mission mainly concerned about "social betterment."[9] Today, for instance, in mostly secular areas of America, man has taken center stage. Freedom, equality, justice, autonomy and other similar

---

[7] Timothy Yates, *Christian Mission in the Twentieth Century* (New York, NY: Cambridge University Press, 1994), 197.

[8] Ibid. 197; http://krestaintheafternoon.blogspot.com/2010/03/should-world-set-agenda.html (Accessed on October 16, 2014).

[9] Ibid.

virtues are highly encouraged, averred, and propagated in every aspect of the social life. These are commendable virtues by themselves, yet they have become idols. Indeed, these cultural emphases were formulated against the backdrop of the old Imperialist British Monarchy, but these days, people have hyper-focused on these values and brought them into the realm of religion, wanting to be free from God, His Church, and His Word. Anything that goes against "my freedom" should get out of my way, including the Mighty God. Thus the rules and standards of God are being abrogated in favor of the standards of men who say: "You should not tell me what is best for *me*. I do not want you to intrude into *my* physical, emotional, intellectual or physical space, especially with your religious talk." The church in the West has heard this individualistic and worldly message for so long that she has accepted it as the norm. The world has set her agenda: whether to preach or not. So she mutters the Gospel for herself and cops out of her Great Commission task, settling for *just* doing her humanitarian work instead of carrying out her priestly mandate.

The parameters for being good and enlightened in Western culture include recycling, eating gluten free, having sophisticated taste in music and movies, not speaking against sexual "preferences," encouraging people to choose abortion, staying up on the latest celebrity gossip (even under the guise of mocking and criticizing the rich and famous), hanging out at a local organic fair trade coffee shop, buying jewelry made by women rescued from sex trafficking, tending a garden and mowing your yard before the grass gets to a centimeter, doing yoga, curating a great image on various social media platforms, sleeping around and bragging about it to friends, avoiding any discussion regarding religion except talking about aliens, astrology and New Age philosophy without imposing any ideas. If you do these things, you are a good, enlightened, tolerant citizen. A few of these things mentioned above can be positive, and it might sound like I am caricaturing unbelieving postmodern Americans – and of course I am to make a point – but the reality is that many people are following the cultural herd in the good things and the bad things like unquestioning sheep with brains on autopilot, even in the church.

I think it is against this background that we should discuss our issue of preaching versus social work. This external postmodern worldview has not only made inroads into the Church; it has also unwittingly affected the beliefs and practices of the believers in the West. In order to align the Church with the world, trying to look good in the eyes of the watching critical masses, the church has loosened its grip on the Gospel. How? Churches are now trying to be good by *just* helping the homeless, feeding the hungry, doing after school care, assisting refugees, doing food pantries and food co-ops and other benevolent supports. They are trying to display their goodness and also somewhat Christ's love through deeds, but silently, without words, because the popular culture insists that speaking of religion is bad, intolerant, and is imposing one's individual view on others, which in their opinion is ignorance and backwardness.

But this begs the question: how is the church different from the world? Christopher Hitchens, Richard Dawkins, Oprah Winfrey, rock stars, and Hollywood movie stars also encourage good deeds like supporting the oppressed, speaking on behalf of the poor and donating millions of dollars to the have-nots. But how is the church of Christ, who is also expected to love her neighbor, supposed to be unique from atheists or unbelievers who do the same or even better deeds? Now as you can detect I am addressing the favorite side of most American churches and most missiologists – Holism – which neglects, foregoes, and waters down the preaching of the Gospel. As

I mentioned earlier, I am an African who believes in the inseparability of the preaching of Christ and love in action, but I cannot be silent when I see the most important aspect of the evangelical faith being thrown out of the window of my host country's Church. I cannot be quiet when the pulpit becomes barren of the Gospel. I know what lacking looks like. I know what poverty is. I know what suffering is, but I can tell you that a piece of clothing or a bundle of money or a full stomach did not give me hope in those moments of need. Rather, the preached word and the hope I embraced through it sustained me.

Above all, I want to mention what my South Sudanese pastor friend said on this matter. After going through fire, in the shadow of death, facing multiple unspeakable losses, walking on thorns and thistles, he still smiled being full of the Lord's joy, and said: "God is good, my brother!" And at another time he said to his congregation while encouraging them to share the Gospel in America: "We have no silver and gold, but we have the Gospel to give to America!"

Did you hear that? Most churches these days, if they lost what they have in their bank account, their property, all the hymn books, the old organ, the new bass guitar and drums, the loudspeakers, would they still preach the Gospel? Would they say the same things my pastor friend said and continue to do the work of evangelists? I doubt that because now for too many mission is *just* doing after-school care, buying blankets for refugees from an African country or feeding the homeless. This is disturbing. Certainly, the church needs to care for the physical needs of people, but not *only* their physical needs. The problem in our day is that the physical has overpowered the spiritual, and we have fattened many to be slaughtered at the *Parousia*.

But I do not lose hope, because the Spirit of God is at work in his scattered people of the Diaspora, who are here in the West for such a time as this. He has trained many through seminaries of suffering in the Red Zone of South Sudan, the tumult of Congo, and the Boko Haram controlled areas of Nigeria. He has prepared many through the school of poverty and lack, giving courses like "Praising When Food, Money or Health Is Absent." There are many faithful Diaspora people here in America who scoff at "success theology" and "the prosperity Gospel" because they intimately know the God who has been with them even in the shadow of death. They know they have come through fire and water only by His grace and strength which has been made perfect in their weakness. They have no gold or silver, but they do have the simple, powerful Gospel: "Sin kills! Satan is real, but Jesus saves! Are you born again?" Indeed, they are here as the have-nots to preach to the haves that they don't have the one thing that is most vital. They are not shy to talk about religion. It is not and has never been offensive to them to talk about God. He is everywhere: in their languages, lives, songs and conversations. This "intrusive" worldview, this assertive God-talk, will, Lord-willing, shake off the worldly decorations which have been put on the American Church of Christ, and it will bring enthusiastic, multi-ethnic, *evangelistic* faith and preaching to America, the 21st century mission field. Through all of this, I hope and pray that the tragic vision of the 1968 World Council of Churches will diminish, because the Church will set the goal for the world, not vice versa.

Indeed, these brothers and sisters, God's new mission force, will make mistakes, yet they will bring the Gospel to the forefront again by doing away with the anthropocentric social club mentality and practices that have become so popular in the Western Church in recent years. They will preach the Gospel *and* they will depict love in action. They will explain why they do good deeds. They won't allow *just* good deeds to suffocate them and take over and burn them out. They will preach repentance and the forgiveness of sins, focusing on transformation from the inside out rather than from the outside in. Their boldness will put off political correctness in obedience to the Great Commission. They will challenge the current silent messengers who have shut their mouths and closed their Bibles for the sake of politics or football. They won't have the will or the power to hide and hoard the Gospel because of the rushing wind of the Spirit through their mouths.

7
Obstacles for Diaspora Cross-Cultural Evangelists

So far, we have seen some obstacles like disunity, lack of language acquisition, church splitting and others as deterring factors for Diaspora cross-cultural evangelism. But here I would like to focus more on aspects of the evangelists' or ministers' personal lives and their milieu that is causing them to stumble and crippling them from becoming effective cross-cultural witnesses in the Diaspora. The obstacles I am going to discuss here are closely connected to each other but I will reflect on them individually to see how each stems from the other.

The first obstacle most Diaspora Christians or evangelists encounter is lack of cross-cultural skills. The evangelist or the African Christian who comes to live, work and minister in the Diaspora might have had a blossoming ministry among his people or even among a people from a similar culture back home, but when he makes a great leap and changes continents to dwell in Europe, or America, it is likely that he has not had the skills that he needs to be an effective cross-cultural preacher or minister. Thus he might not know how to interact with others from a totally different culture. He might feel like a baby who is bewildered by his new environment. He might feel helpless and at a loss. Consequently, he fails to understand the culture he has encountered. He misses the cues, the worldviews and the systems with which the new culture functions. This in turn leads him to be frustrated and feel useless in a foreign land. He likely will become depressed as no one seems to understand his pain, struggle and dilemma. He contemplates going back to his hometown as soon as possible.

At times, for he expects everyone to be the same as people from his own culture, he will be offended at some of the expressions, gestures and brief conversations of the locals or immigrants from other cultures. He will overreact both to good and bad situations because he is neither in control of, nor understanding of his new and unique milieu. But if he had had cross-cultural skills that he acquired through orientation or some sort of training before or at his arrival, if he had known the worldview the culture is functioning from, and if he had known and had been exposed gradually to various cultures and taught how to exegete the culture and appreciate diversity, his experience would have been much better in the Diaspora.

The second obstacle the cross-cultural evangelist faces in his ministry in the Diaspora is lack of intentionality. The evangelist or an ordinary Christian needs to pray for an open door for the Gospel to cross-cultural boundaries so that he can convey the Gospel to people different from him. But the answer to this prayer will not be realized unless the believer – the Diaspora evangelist – seizes every opportunity. Instead of only talking to people that he knows, why does he not strike up a conversation at Starbucks, saying, "Nice day, huh?" or, commenting to the guy in line at Walmart or Goodwill, saying "It's cheaper here, I like shopping here." Making these kind of friendly statements is a clue in American culture that someone wants to talk. By the way, Americans put their guard down when they hear your accent and they are generally interested to exchange a few words even if they are not interested to talk to you for long. Trust me, it works. I have done it multiple times. They will ask, "Where are you from?" I say, "Ethiopia." And the American might say, "I am sorry about my geography, but is it in West Africa?" Then

I tell them that it is found in East Africa while being careful not to insult their intelligence. Usually my conversation ends up moving into spiritual matters because the topic of my recent studies (Theology) usually comes up. The point is this: be intentional in every situation so that Christ may be known. It took me a while to be intentional in the Diaspora. I had no clue about the culture at first. But with the help of my wife and other believers, I was able to attain that mindset for Christ's glory. Many of my Diaspora friends from Africa indeed struggle with this. There are a number of distractions and detours to being intentional to make Christ known.

The third obstacle a Diaspora believer faces in cross-cultural ministry is loneliness. It is an undeniable fact that the West is ultra-individualistic and explicitly postmodern. The Diaspora Gospel workers, who have come from a communal society that celebrates sharing, extended meetings, and unstructured and unlimited face-to-face conversation, has been challenged, appalled and affected by it. This environment, especially in the West, has driven many immigrants to withdrawal, bitterness, depression, grumbling, flagrant sins and suicide. Recently an old man from my neighboring country was found dead in his house and nobody knew about it until a few weeks later. If this was in his country he would have been buried on the same or the next day. Because of the me-centered, secluded life in the West, many Africans have embraced the media as a way of escape. Some watch TV or movies 24-7. At least it helps them temporarily forget the piercing pain of their unmet need to socialize and be human. The fast-paced, individualistic culture that highlights individual rights, comfort and personal freedom has killed the communal, passionate Africans' zeal in preaching the Gospel to their neighbors. Individualism has not benefited the Westerners themselves, let alone the Africans. As I mentioned, it has driven many to addictions and suicide. It has created lack of accountability and disseminated the idea of selfishness and self-absorption. This dismal aspect of Western society has crippled gifted preachers, prayer warriors and evangelists from Africa, preventing them from becoming effective cross-cultural workers. In order to combat this, I believe Diaspora believers should learn how the people in the host culture meet and socialize in order to share the Gospel in a relevant way. We, as Africans, need to pick up the cues and grasp the system people are operating in if we hope to lead many to the community of God. These days many of those who seem to glory in individualism are actually hungry for relationships, meaningful and extended face-to-face time with others. They are struggling with depression and anxiety because they lack relationships with God as well as with their neighbor.

The fourth obstacle is sexual sin. The African Christian worker inevitably will face the pervasive sex-saturated world of the West. Before I go further it is appropriate for me to make a caveat. Sexual immorality is found everywhere. And one can see the consequence of that in the HIV/AIDS epidemic we have in Africa. But does that mean the West is less immoral? Certainly not. Here I am addressing more of the availability as well as the integration of sexuality in every aspect of life in the West.

The billboards, the internet, the TV and movies, and the magazines have made sex and sexuality the omnipresent god in the West. A farmer from Ethiopia or a young high school girl from Somalia or an effective preacher from Congo coming to the States will all be confronted by that. Many immigrants have not previously had a TV in their house or a readily available internet connection. But now they are here and everything is a click away. Eyes that are not trained, hearts that are not prepared, minds that are not desensitized are now encircled, exposed and vulnerable. As a result, sexual addiction has blindsided and overpowered many Diaspora cross-cultural evangelists. Lust has entangled many. This is a tragedy, for lust slowly kills us and also makes us so unmissional. It disables us from becoming effective cross-cultural workers. I am going to be honest, I have struggled. Praise God, I took the advice of godly men and took practical steps to counteract the bait of Satan, so he did not devour me as he wanted to. Small bites of lust can take chunks of our spiritual progress and passion. We must not be unaware of Satan's schemes. One cannot become an effective cross-cultural worker if he is stung by lust, because lust fills him with shame, regrets, and dirt, and makes the evangelist focus on himself and not others.

My dear African brothers need to seek someone to be their accountability partner, not just when sin is committed but before it happens. This would protect them from running to the TV, internet, depression or sin. It would create an healthy environment where they would be encouraged and nurtured so that they could become effective cross-cultural Diaspora evangelists by overcoming any barriers. Thus they would say no to the suggestive oversexed culture that adores the sex-centered lifestyle and keep sex in its intended place: under the gaze and guidance of the God who created it.

The fifth obstacle for the cross-cultural Diaspora evangelist is materialism. The have-nots long to have and the haves always want to have more. Materialism is like "the leech [that] has two daughters [who cry constantly] 'give' and 'give'... [They are like] Sheol, the barren womb, the land never satisfied with water, and the fire that never says, 'enough'" (Pro. 30:15-16). Buying, shopping, and buying and again shopping and cramming more and more material things into daily life is the rule of the day in the world but most evidently in the United States. The temporal has become the central. People are defined by their possessions, and the church is entrapped with this state of life.

Materialism is part of the reason some contemporary mission theologians – whether Holists or preachers of success and prosperity – have elevated helping the poor. Materialism is the reason the preaching of Christ has faded away in favor of caring *just* for the physique and the excessive accumulation of material things at the expense of the saving Gospel. At least the Holists are better than the success theologians and preachers. The previous ones strive to bring the American Dream to the Majority World or even to their own people to make them rich – if not saved – but ends up creating dependency, whereas the latter ones try to make themselves rich at the expense of the poor. In the end, however, both are materialists. Both attach the believer or the believer-to-be to the world and produce disciples who are shallow and worldly. What would you expect from a "Christian" who is bribed into the religion? He came for and because of material gain and he will continue live and die for it. When there is no more material benefit he will leave for Corinth like Demas (2 Tim. 4:10). Materialist missionaries seem whole but they have holes, they talk about success but they do not know that they have failed.

Now most of the Diaspora community of God is ensnared by the appeal of materialism. For example, Christmas is about me, myself and I getting material things. Life is all about me experiencing the American dream. It is all about what I have accumulated. I live for it. I labor for it. I even die for it. Life is about the car I drive, the home I own, the kind of flatscreen TV or laptop I possess. Spiritual life, "seek first the kingdom of God and his righteousness, and all these things will be added to you" (Matt. 6:33), is reversed. "[N]o longer I...but Christ" (Gal. 2:20), is now "no longer Christ but I and the things I own!" How incredibly sad!

African communities, including cross-cultural workers, are too often numbed by the poison of materialism. That communal mentality and those sharing practices of their home cultures have evaporated and been replaced by a self-centered hoarding mentality. Diaspora cross-cultural ministers need to forgo the televangelists' appeal and the holist's approach and preach to themselves and others the genuine sacrificial Gospel. I am not advocating a poverty mentality. Having more is not necessarily bad. We make a fatal error, however, when we make what we have the center of our life, a source of pride, and something that we live and die for.

The sixth and last obstacle is busyness. Busyness is a huge challenge among the Diaspora community. They have to work hard, day and night, so as to provide for themselves as well as for the family back home. Most people in the Diaspora community have labor-intensive jobs which cause inevitable exhaustion. Most go to church or do ministry in their tiny windows of extra time with hardly any energy left in them. I cannot ignore the commitment of most Diaspora believers when they show up at church after demanding and dreary work hours to worship their God.[10] Cross-cultural ministry in the Diaspora requires patience, flexibility and fervent prayer so as to be effective in the little amount of time available for ministry. It is also vital to have a team of cross-cultural ministers who could be available for evangelistic ministry as well as edifying ministry within the church to maximize the effectiveness of the community's ministry in the society at large. There are a number of Diaspora Christians who do not go to any church, let alone engage in a cross-cultural evangelistic ministry, because of soul-crushing busyness. The existing Diaspora Church needs to come up with a conducive plan for incorporating these brothers and

---

[10]Emmanuel Gospel Center, "The East African Church in New England."

sisters into a local church and to equip and send them to be effective cross-cultural witnesses in the marketplace.

8
Critical Engagement in Diaspora Cross-Cultural Evangelism

We have seen in the previous chapter that one of the obstacles of a cross-cultural witness in the Diaspora is lack of cross-cultural skills. But I want to delve more deeply into one area that needs to be emphasized for such a ministry among African believers in general and African cross-cultural evangelists and ministers in particular.

There are two general dispositions the Diaspora Christians fall into when it comes to their attitude in engaging the Western culture: **the West is the best** or **the West is the worst**. Both are dangerous dispositions that stem from plain naïveté. These dispositions need to be addressed and be brought to the correct perspective and reality; otherwise it will affect the way these Diaspora Christians and their ministers do cross-cultural evangelism in the West. Let us examine each extreme and then the biblical middle way.

Those who hold to the idea that the West is the best are usually those who went through a lot and grew tired of their own culture, government, economy, religion and country. This could happen to any Diaspora person, whether an Animist, Christian or Muslim. For example, the author of *Infidel*, Ayaan Hirsi Ali, would fall under such a category. Others manifest this disposition by stating that there is nothing good in their culture, country or continent, thus expressing "Afro-pessimism."[11] They insist that

---

[11] Afro-pessimism used in Tite Tienou's article is mainly done by non-Africans who paint "the negative image of Africa and Africans" but here I used it to show that it is also used by Africans themselves. Tite Tienou, "Integrity of Mission in Light of the Gospel in Africa: A perspective from an African Diaspora" in *Mission Studies* 24 (Leiden: Koninklijke Brill NV, 2007), 219.

change is not going to happen in their home cultures – ever! Thus they recant and renounce everything they have known and embrace everything the West has to provide. They throw themselves at the bosom of the West without the slightest hesitation or consideration. They are blind to some of the good things that are found in their own culture. They are also blind to some of the negative cultural practices and beliefs found in their host culture.

Diaspora believers who are fatigued by war, tribalism, unstructured church polity, poverty and other maladies are quick to ignore the good in their own background. They display bitterness, hatred and disgust towards the culture of their origin. Their solution is to embrace their host culture with lack of critical engagement. I have met many from every walk of life who depict such an attitude. My Somali friend states that her country is a mess and so there is no hope, no good in her culture. My Ethiopian friend who is doing his doctoral studies could not see the good in our culture, thus he disparages it at every opportunity yet he uncritically admires and adores the American culture. My Nigerian friend could only see pitch dark things in his culture, to the point that he has no positive words, not a single one, concerning his culture specifically and other African countries' cultures in general. My Namibian friend cannot see the goodness of his culture, because it only gives attention to older people not the young ones like him even though he is thirty-something. Thus he throws away the good treasures in his culture because there are some problems. My dear friend from Central African Republic detests his culture. "They do not apply binary logic, they are not as logical as Americans and they lack discipleship," he says. Discipleship, for him, is only the problem of the African church. Because in the West, of course, *everyone* is a good disciple, right? I could go on and on. Here my friends are suffering from that lack of critical engagement of their own as well as their host culture, throwing the baby out with the bath water in one instance while naively gulping the bath water of the new culture without hesitation. Because they are not able to see where sin and Satan are affecting Western culture, these Diaspora believers have trouble communicating the Gospel.

The other extreme disposition asserts that the West is the worst. All Americans are racist, so carnal and irreligious, it says. The Hollywood movies are these Diaspora people's primary source of knowledge for what the West looks like. What they see in the West is all wrong and only *their* culture is good pure, and correct. They feel that their culture is the only one God ordained and made and that it is too flawless to have any problems. They are oblivious to the fact that their own culture is full of flaws and that it is far from being heavenly. As a result, they do not have close friends from the host culture. They live as hermits – a way of escapism – to protect themselves from the impurity, filth and corruption of the host culture. But the irony is that they consume Hollywood's offerings or what the Western TV and Internet provides in their solitude. But then they have that disgusted look when they see a person or talk about an individual from the Western host culture.

They think they could find nothing good because the West represents everything bad to them. This disposition has made a number of Diaspora believers become secluded and insulated. Fear of becoming stained or corrupted has crippled the Diaspora community, preventing them from becoming cross-cultural disciple makers of their host-culture neighbors. Thus they are unable to carry out the mission they are supposed to fulfill.

So what should be done to change such extreme and mission-killing dispositions? What should be the proper attitude and approach for the Diaspora community of God to become effective cross-cultural witnesses? Well, there is a *via media*, a middle way: critical engagement.

Critical engagement is a discerning disposition that allows one to see the right from wrong, the good from the bad. This is a disposition that allows the cross-cultural evangelist in the Diaspora to be intentional, missional and humble. It allows him to be a realist who is able to see his culture and tell you that he appreciates some parts of it and disapproves of some of them. He sees that God has created cultures, sin has corrupted them and we, as God's ambassadors, can engage, challenge, and redeem them. He does not dismiss a culture just because it is different from his. He admires and worships God for the beauty through diversity. He also groans and bemoans the fact that all cultures always strive to suppress God and invent their own gods. He weighs every culture against the Word of God, engages it so that he could make the name and work of Christ known in that specific culture. He engages it critically because after all it is not all about his likes or dislikes but about preaching Christ, the crucified, among the nations.

9
Ethnocentrism:
the Universal Plague in the Diaspora

As an Ethiopian, I think I should begin by focusing on myself and my countrymen critically in regard to ethnocentrism. Ethiopians, like many cultures and people, are prideful, and feel superior over others, including over Europeans and Americans. Having received the earliest church tradition in the fourth century, defeating the Italians twice and then becoming the only non-colonized African country except Liberia, who was a country of free slaves, having our own alphabet and calendar, ancient world-class churches and obelisks, etc., have become a source of pride – at times arrogance – for Ethiopians. Some Ethiopians, according to my coworker in the harvest from West Africa, refer to themselves as Ethiopians and other Africans as "the Africans!" This is mostly the general nationwide perspective, but if one ever goes deeper inside Ethiopia, people are even more ethnocentric. Ethiopians, like the Somalis, Rwandese or Nigerians, are tribe-conscious even toward their countrymen.[12]

We can see many vivid examples of the consequences of ethnocentrism in Africa: the two major Rwandese tribes' recent fate, the Civil War in Kenya a few years ago, the stateless country Somalia and the newborn state of South Sudan, which have both disintegrated into clans and sub clans, to name only a few.

When Africans cross cultures and move to other countries and continents they not only pack their passport and unique souvenirs from their beloved area but also their tribal mentality. It

---

[12] Emmanuel Gospel Center, "The East African Church in New England."

is not something that can be left at some place before flying to the United States or Holland. It is embedded in the mind, the heart, and the soul – the whole being. Thus it is no surprise to see the African Christian Diaspora reflecting such a state of mind in the church and ministry.

This plague is not confined to Africans alone. Americans, both blacks and whites, have struggled with it even after the Civil Rights movement. Some of the people who go to our continent tell us to love our neighbors and are appalled by the existence of tribalism in Africa, but they fail to do the same with their Hispanic or African-American or American Indian neighbors. At times, I wish to ask them how many friends from other cultures they have. Koreans also look down upon Chinese, the mainland Chinese feel superior over the Taiwanese, the Malays over the Filipinos and Indonesians, the Japanese over other Asians, and many Asians detest the Japanese.[13] Ethnocentrism has used the Bible and the Koran as proof texts. It has used history for justification and retribution. It has used economics to undermine others, governments to take advantage of the "inferiors," and science (like Darwinism) to exterminate the weaklings, the unfit and the unwanted.

Ethnocentrism is an innate attitudinal poison, but it builds its muscle through others' influence, bad experiences or successes, historical scars, injustice, revenge, hatred, etc. Even those who consider themselves enlightened, tolerant, and defenders of the poor, the weak and the oppressed have this poison ingrained in their whole person. They might not show their ethnocentrism explicitly but it might ooze out when it gains an opportune time.

---

[13] Spirit-filled, changed believers like Korean-American Dr. Michael Oh who serves in Japan, have gone against the contours by showing the love of Christ regardless of historical atrocities done to their families and their countries by the Japanese government.

Returning to the African Christian Diaspora, this is a huge issue among brothers and sisters from my continent. They (including myself) struggle with this issue, though in various degrees. Ethnocentrism has made many try to replicate their village from back home and become aloof to others including some other tribes from their own motherland. They have a country within their own country. Coming to the West has made it even worse. The clinging is far stronger. Loving one's country and more specifically one's own ethnicity, language, and customs is not wrong in itself, but the problem comes when one prioritizes one's ethnicity over making disciples of other nations or displays explicit or implicit superiority and rejection of another's ethnicity, language and culture. When one clings to one's own ethnicity to the ignorance of, rejection of, and indifference to another's ethnicity, that person is forgetting and rejecting the fact that God has made all ethnicities out of one man (Acts 17:26). It is rejecting, denying and ignoring the Creator's design. Not only that, but it is also renouncing the mandate, which is His mandate, of crossing cultural boundaries to help other cultures know and glorify God the Father, the Son and the Holy Spirit.[14]

Besides, it depicts the lack of that deeper yet simple understanding of the fact that the Gospel is not supposed to be bound by our preferences. It should not be confined within the four walls of a single ethnicity. To allow this is to be greedy, a vicious hoarder of the revealed grace of God, withholding love from others who are different from us, which directly goes against the command to love our neighbors (Lev. 19:18; Mark 12:31; Jas. 2:8). But apart from the universal fall of humanity, what other things are

---

[14] cf. Christopher R. Little, "ICS 6030: Biblical Theology of Mission" (Lecture, Columbia International University Seminary and Graduate School of Ministry, Columbia, SC, 2013).

contributing to this persistent debilitating stance of African Diaspora Christians, and what can militate against such an attitude so that these new forces in the West might become effective in obedience to the call for cross-cultural discipleship?

I think there are three causes for ethnocentrism in any community, particularly for African Christ followers. The first one is the fact that most are here because of the other ethnic majorities' or even minorities' oppression. Take for instance Sudan. Most Sudanese are in the Diaspora because the Arab Sudanese persecuted, oppressed and undermined the South Sudanese. As a result, they are dispersed everywhere. This would force the exiles to trust their own people, the persecuted majority in general and then their own clan specifically. Or take the Somalis: though they proclaim that they have "one language, one religion and one ethnicity," they are deeply divided into four or five clans. Somalis are dispersed all over the world because of ethnocentrism, but also because of Euro-American, Russian and regional aggression, they claim. Thus they are embittered toward each respective culture. Besides, their religion inhibits many from intermingling with "unbelievers." Whatever the justification or pretext, they also suffer from a deeply embedded ethnocentrism. For example, clan members send money to support their clan in fighting the other clan members in the homeland.[15]

The second cause for ethnocentrism among the Diaspora is globalization. One might think that because the world is becoming one village through the internet, homogeneity is inevitable. Indeed, it is true if the homogeneity is referring to having the same news or

---

[15] Ahmed Ali Haile, *Teatime in Mogadishu: My Journey As a Peace Ambassador in the World of Islam*, as told to David W. Shenk (Harrisonburg, VA: Herald Press, 2011), 100-101; Mazie Hough, "Why Now? A Brief History of Somalia" in *Somalis in Maine: Cross-Cultural Currents*, ed. Kimberly A. Huisman et al. (Berkley, CA: North Atlantic Books, 2011), 7-22; Ayaan Hirsi Ali, *Infidel* (New York, NY: Atria Paper Back, 2007).

information access within a microsecond throughout the globe. But it is a mere naïveté to assume that everyone has one culture and worldview because of this. Globalization has made and is making even more militant ethnocentrists, positively as well as negatively. Positively, in the face of pervasive globalization that is challenging and eliminating diversity and uniqueness, most Diasporas are being awakened to the fact that tomorrow they might lose their cultural treasures and identity, thus they are working hard at keeping them intact. This is depicted particularly in their efforts to nurture their children in their language, culture, religion and customs. Look at afterschool programs run at Diaspora churches or mosques, or the insistence of parents speaking to their children in Dinka, Amharic or Somali. It is a fight against homogeneity, against *monoculturalism*: the hidden creed and the goal of postmodernism. One can see the paradox that globalization is trying to nurture, the lack of absoluteness in any form, thus advocating multiculturalism, that at the same time it is driving cultures to become one culture. The Diaspora believers, knowingly or unknowingly, have become aware of this threat to their culture. They are afraid of losing it. So they struggle, they fight as they fought against the ethnic cleansing in Rwanda or Darfur or Mogadishu. But the struggle to maintain their identity in their voluntary or involuntary exiles has taken many African Diasporas to the other extreme. Though their children are fluent in multiple languages, as opposed to the parents themselves, they are taught implicitly or explicitly that others are different and inferior while their culture is superior.

A non-Christian African Diaspora from East Africa was recently complaining to me about how the North Americans, especially the young ones (interestingly, the postmodern ones), are racist. He told me with disgust and even hatred that they do not treat the Blacks, whether Somalis or Ethiopians, equally. But to my amazement, this same friend of mine was looking down upon his African neighbors from West Africa. He was blind to his double standard. When he named the names of their countries you could see how he considered them inferior and lowly.

Some others, because they do not personally spend time with people from different cultures, have misinformation about other ethnicities. They get their information from the media, which has its own agenda and bias. For instance, one lady I met from a neighboring country of Ethiopia was talking about another people group from another country. She told me that these people are "liars, cheaters and wild!" I asked "Really? Why is that?" Then she started telling me various reasons and how they lacked manners. And she added, "But us, we are very different. We do not lie. We do not have the guts to cheat in broad daylight." To this I asked, "How did you know about their cheating and lying? Did you work with them in a shop or an office?" My Diaspora friend stated, "I read about them in the newspaper!" Then I was able to see clearly that she had no idea what she was talking about. She was discipled by the media, the American newspaper! The area was a bit biased towards the people she was talking about. So it was easy to know how she had become biased and started to feel superior towards these people. Finally I had to tell her that these people are lost and as a result we should not expect them not to lie or cheat, if they are indeed doing that. And I insisted that they needed the Gospel to change.

The third reason for ethnocentrism in the Diaspora community is the yearning for one's country or village, so to speak. There is a popular saying among the Diaspora, "Home is always home!"

Though they have relative comfort, material goods and modernity, their souls yearn to where they grew up, where they lived, worked and married. They miss their motherland. This is normal and human. The Psalmist is also heard yearning for his hometown, his past ministry and glory while he was somewhere as an exile Diaspora (Psalm 42:4). Daniel prayed, begged and interceded when he found out the nearness of the completion of the 70 years exile, so as to return to his homeland (Dan. 9:1-19). Ezra, Nehemiah and Zerubbabel led the ones who yearned to go back to their homeland (Ezra 2:1-70; 8:1-36; Neh. 7:5-65). The Israelites were also collectively in such a state of longing (Psa. 137), but this normal longing has the potential to make one a separatist, and ethnocentric person. Too much thinking and longing for their homeland might urge the Diaspora believers to put their cross-cultural evangelism on the back burner. And if their going back does not happen or if they persist in such a state of mind, they will inevitably become victims of depression. Thus they will not be able to proclaim the Gospel joyfully across cultures, for they will be obsessed in dealing with their own melancholic state of affairs!

Then what is the solution for ethnocentrism? How shall a Diaspora believer from Africa overcome this insidious flaw? It is vital to know, first of all, that one cannot change oneself. Thus the intervention of the Holy Spirit is vital. The Diaspora believer has to *admit* to the fact that he is plagued with this universal poison. And then he should *bring* this problem to God so that He can work on his heart, to change his attitude, and to give him an open mind to appreciate other cultures. If there is any past hurt because of ethnocentric causes like personal conflict, historical and political scars, or economic and religious oppression carried out by other ethnicities, he needs to *ask* for the healing of God, then for the ability and opportunity to be reconciled to people from those specific ethnicities. Diaspora cross-cultural opportunities will come when the believer intentionally tries to *make* friends from ethnicities other than his own. Maintaining ties to one's own ethnicity, worshiping in his language or planting churches for his own people group is not a sin or wrong. As a pastor, though, he can encourage some gifted cross-cultural evangelists to cross cultures and provide them with resources that they need for the effectiveness of their ministry. For non-pastors, just befriending others, having coffee together, playing soccer or board games is a possibility, and trying to learn the basics of their languages is commendable.

Diaspora Christians can also study books of the Bible like Acts, Esther, Daniel, and Revelation, so that they understand that God is the designer of all cultures. They should also learn about other cultures (especially the host culture) so that they will be able to understand and help their multilingual and multicultural children. In doing so, they inculcate the appreciation of cultures and discernment of various worldviews so that they can appreciate or reject aspects of any culture based on the teachings of Scripture.

Other remedies for ethnocentrism as well as lack of cross-cultural connections could be that leaders of various ethnic or country or language-based churches can speak at each others' churches.[16] This will strengthen the congregations' exposure to interact with people different from them in many respects. When leaders of such congregations lead the way, the remaining members of the church will follow. Hence, leaders or pastors or elders are setting a model to be replicated. Attending ethnic festivals and

---

[16] This might require an introducer, a middle man so that it would happen smoothly. Jessica A. Udall, "Ethiopian Immigrants as Cross-Cultural Missionaries: Activating the Diaspora for Great Commission Impact" (paper presented at the annual meeting for the Evangelical Missiological Society, Atlanta, Georgia, September 25-27, 2014).

bazaars would also help believers learn about various cultures, peoples and countries. New Year's celebrations, independence days, and other significant days (at times discretion might be vital when attending ceremonies or events as such since they might be asked to do things that would violate their commitment to the Bible and their faith) could be some of the gatherings they might want to attend. Birthdays, weddings, and funerals are also opportune times to make friends, learn who unbelievers are and be a bridge for them to be reconciled to Christ through the sharing of the Word and the demonstration of their genuine love, kindness and interest. Watching historical, geographical and cultural documentaries could also help to educate themselves with regard to others' cultures and customs. But they might want to verify the truthfulness of the stories told in those documentaries with real people from the respective cultures or countries, since some have their own agenda in making those documentaries. Most of the time, the media presents a modified, caricatured or even twisted version of others' countries or cultures and identities. For example, most international students are afraid of American big cities because of the action movies they've watched. Or most Muslims believe that everyone in the US is Christian and that all of them (especially girls) act like people in Hollywood movies and porn stars. Or everyone in Ethiopia, Kenya or Somalia is hungry. All these stereotypes are due to lack of exposure to people and overexposure to mass media and their selective, biased and one-sided story line.

A Biblical Paradigm for the Diaspora Community

These all died in faith, not having received the things promised, but having seen them and greeted them from afar, and having acknowledged that they were strangers and exiles on the earth. For people who speak thus make it clear that they are seeking a homeland. If they had been thinking of that land from which they had gone out, they would have had opportunity to return. But as it is, they desire a better country, that is, a heavenly one. Therefore God is not ashamed to be called their God, for he has prepared for them a city (Heb. 11:13-16).

I thought my reflection on Diaspora cross-cultural evangelism had ended in the previous chapter. Thus I closed my notebook and put away my pen and was engaged in editing the previous chapters, until I stumbled upon Hebrews 11:13-16 during my devotional time. It dawned on me that most of the faithful people listed in chapter eleven were Diasporas, for they were identified as "strangers and exiles" in Canaan, Egypt, and Babylon.

As I read the text and observed, I was stunned at how the Diaspora men and women of God – "a cloud of witnesses" (Heb. 12:1) – lived as believers in foreign lands. Though they were from various periods and milieus, they followed similar principles and lifestyles throughout the history of redemption. This is pointed out to us by the all-encompassing and inclusive expressions, "These all" and "All these" (Heb. 11:13, 39). All those mentioned in this passage operated under a universal and timeless paradigm as Diaspora men and women of God. So what was their paradigm?

Dying in Faith: The Goal of Faithful Diaspora

First, the author makes it clear: "These all died in faith." To whom does "[t]hese all" refer? Indeed, the immediate context of Hebrews 11:13-16 indicates that it is referring to all the people that the author mentioned from verse 4 through 11; that is, Abel to Sarah. But a close observation of the text, as well as the phrase "All these" in verse 39 indicates that the wider context includes everyone mentioned in the whole chapter and even those whom the author could not mention because "Time is too short for me to tell" (Heb. 11:32). They "all died in faith." This statement might not impress us at first unless we continue reading the next phrase: they died "without having received the promises." The weight of dying in faith becomes vivid when one recalls the situations that "[t]hese all" passed through: various trials and difficulties as Diasporas. Since "[t]ime is too short for me to tell about" all the men and women mentioned in chapter 11, I will focus on the few who were outside of their physical homeland: Abraham, Jacob, Joseph, Moses and Daniel.

Abraham was sent by God to a foreign land that he did not know; he had no child for decades upon decades, and when he received a son after waiting for so long, he was asked to sacrifice him. He did not inherit the land that was promised to him. He did not see how he could be the father of the nations with just two sons. But despite these facts, he was faithful and full of faith and "died in faith." This does not mean he did not doubt or struggle. While living in a foreign land as God's emissary, he was afraid that a stranger was going to succeed him (Gen. 15:2), he lied to preserve his life and gave away his wife (Gen. 12:10-20; 20:1-13), and he slept with a woman that was not his wife because of the impatience of his wife and himself in waiting on God for a child (Gen. 16:1-4). Regardless of his weaknesses and doubts, however, he was a faithful Diaspora.

Jacob, was another Diaspora who "died in faith." He received the same promise as his father Isaac and his grandfather Abraham. Yet, he himself did not receive the promise of land, nation and fame. In fact he experienced famine and he had to go down to Egypt along with his family. But he believed in God and his promises. He had faith that God would bring his promises to fulfillment through his children and grandchildren. Hence he blessed them by faith while he was on his deathbed (Gen. 49:1-33).

Joseph, the proclaimer of God's power and might in a foreign land, did not have an easy life. Having been sold into slavery by his jealous brothers, he went down to Egypt. While serving an Egyptian man, he was falsely accused of sexual harassment and then thrown into jail. There he was forgotten by the very men whom he helped. They did not keep their promises to ask for his immediate release. He eventually came to power after interpreting a decisive dream for the pharaoh of Egypt. He faithfully served God as well as the people under his supervision using his God-given gifts. God's people were still in Egypt without a homeland, but Joseph had faith that God would deliver his people and bring them to the Promised Land. Consequently, Joseph insisted that his bones be taken with the Israelites into the Promised Land and be buried there (Gen. 50:24-25; Ex. 13:19; Jos. 24:32). And then he also "died in faith."

Moses was born in a very turbulent time. He was an Egyptian-born Hebrew. The Hebrews were being persecuted and enslaved by the Egyptians. In order to mitigate the growth of the Hebrew population, Pharaoh promulgated that newborn male babies should be killed. But Moses "was hidden for three months by his parents," and therefore, he escaped death (Heb. 11:23). He was adopted and was raised by Pharaoh's daughter. I cannot imagine what was going through his head and heart when he found out that he was a Hebrew living in the house of Pharaoh yet his people were suffering under the Egyptians' rule. When he became old enough, he "refused to be called the son of Pharaoh's daughter" (Heb. 11:24). He identified himself instead with his own people. He eventually ministered among his people and also proclaimed the might of God to the Egyptians and displayed God's power before them. He led God's people out of bondage. Though he did not enter the Promised Land, he was sure that God would fulfill his promises through his protégé, Joshua. And he "died in faith" after looking at the Land from afar.

Daniel became a Diaspora evangelist and prophet through deportation. Before he arrived in Babylon, the Chaldeans destroyed the temple in Jerusalem, killed many people, imprisoned some and exiled many others. While serving in Babylon, life was not smooth for Daniel. He had to struggle to stay pure. His life was threatened because the king decreed that all wise men should be put to death because the king could not remember his dream until God revealed that mystery to Daniel. He was accused by jealous colleagues and was consequently thrown in the den of lions. Nevertheless, Daniel was faithful in that foreign land. He faithfully prayed, studied the Word, and served God and the kings of the land. He employed his God-given gifts to make Yahweh known among the polytheist pagans. He had unswerving faith in God and not in men; as a result, God rescued him from the wild beasts. In the end, he finished well because he "died in faith."

At this point, you might say "so what?" That is really a good question. The 'so what' of this section is that living as a Diaspora is not a smooth life. Whether you are young like Daniel or older like Abraham, educated like Moses and Daniel, or wise like Jacob, or whether you work in a high-up position like Joseph, whether you are in a foreign land voluntarily like Abraham, or because of famine like Jacob and his family, or because of war and deportation like Daniel and his comrades, you should know one thing: you have to keep your faith and be faithful like your forefathers until God keeps his promises. You and I should be faithful until the end. There are inevitable ups and downs while living in a foreign land. If you are part of the Diaspora, you have tasted some of the challenges, and more might come your way as you progress in your faith pilgrimage. But we should remember this: dying in faith is what matters the most. Despite our trials, we should declare God's promises and his faithfulness. We should not forget that these faith giants in the book of Hebrews were faithful even "without having received the promises." Dying in faith is the goal, because it is after death that we shall see God and be in his majestic presence. This is the overarching paradigm for the Diaspora community of God. But in order to achieve this goal, there were some things these faithful Diaspora men and women of God did.

First, the faithful Diaspora men and women of God saw "the promises" and fixed their eyes upon "them." Their faith was not passive but active, for they "greeted them." Their hope sprang up because of God's promises despite their unfavorable situations. They were future-oriented. They were obsessed with eternity without neglecting their call in the here and now. They were not short-sighted; they had a clear vision (Heb. 11:13b, 26-27). They correctly understood where they belonged, and knew there were better things than this present world (Heb. 11:13b, 19-20, 26, 35, 38). They were future-oriented as well as engaged in the present.

Second, they "confessed that they were foreigners and temporary residents on the earth." The verb "confessed" (HCSB), or "acknowledged" (ESV) could preferably be translated as "declared" from the Greek word *homologeō*. The faithful Diaspora servants of God not only saw, greeted and acknowledged the promises, but they also declared that they did not belong here on earth as permanent residents because they had a glimpse of the promised Messiah and their future homeland, where they belonged as citizens. They did not hoard the hope, which was their hope, to themselves. Instead, they continued to "speak [about the promises and] make it clear that they were seeking a homeland" (Heb. 11:14; Gen 23:4; 47:9; Ps. 39:12).

Indeed, they were asking for a plot of ground in a foreign land in the here and now, but ultimately they were also "seeking a homeland....a better country, that is, a heavenly one" (Heb. 11:14, 16). This is a great template for God's contemporary Diaspora in foreign countries. We should declare that we have a permanent dwelling place, a better city, a country that we long to live in without any hassle. We also need to share the hope we have with the hopeless. The source of hope for the "cloud of witnesses" and for us is the Messiah Jesus. We must confess before others that he is preparing a house, a city, a country for us (John 14:3). In order to do this, we might need to learn and understand the foreign culture that we live in like Moses and Daniel, or move out of our comfort zone and trek to the people groups in the present day Canaan like Abraham.

Indeed, Abraham or Moses could have returned to their homeland, but they obeyed God and fulfilled their mission by forgoing that opportunity. Abraham, especially, could have gone back when he missed his kinsmen or when his wife died. Rather, he stayed and finished his race while gazing on the One who had promised to come and dwell among humanity.

As a result of their perseverance in faith in the face of "few and evil...days" (Gen. 47:9), "God is not ashamed to be called their God" (Heb. 11:16b). God was and is their God. They trusted him, obeyed him, declared him and had faith in him. And they were never let down by the Lord. As the Scriptures testify in unison:

"Indeed, none who wait for you shall be put to   shame" (Ps. 25:3).

"Then you will know that I am the LORD; those who wait for me shall not be put to shame" (Isa. 49:23).
"Everyone who believes in him shall not be put to shame"
(Rom. 10:11).

The Diaspora people of God mentioned in the book of Hebrews trusted God; thus he was not ashamed to declare: "'I am the God of Abraham, and the God of Isaac, and the God of Jacob'" (Mark 12:26; cf. Gen 26:24; 28:13). God not only declared himself as their God but "he [also] has prepared for them a city" (Heb. 11:16). The writer of Hebrews points out that God's preparation of a city for the faithful Diaspora of the past was a ratification, a signpost of his unashamedness of his servants in foreign lands. Now they are with him in the heavenly city. They are alive and well in their new homeland living as permanent citizens because "He is not God of the dead, but of the living" (Mark 12:27). This city is also our destination, our eternal fate, but before then we must be steadfast in the faith, incessant proclaimers of our promised permanent home and our hope through the Messiah Jesus that we "saw" and "greeted." May God help us to die in faith as we look for a heavenly country. Indeed, he will.

Study Questions for Group Discussions

Chapter 1:

1. The author says that disunity is a distraction from cross-cultural evangelism. Why do you think this is? In what ways does disunity cause distraction?
2. Why is unity so important for the Church (Jn. 17:1-26)?
3. Why is disunity a particular problem in the Diaspora?
4. What is the principle of Matthew 18:15-35? How does it apply to the situation of disunity among members of the Body of Christ?
5. How can unity be cultivated in the Diaspora Church?

Chapter 2:

1. If you speak more than one language, what is the difference you experience when listening to the Word of God in your native language compared to your second language?
2. Have you considered studying another language for the purpose of ministry? What language would you study if you did?

Chapter 3:

1. What are the characteristics of the Jonah Syndrome that the author talks about?
2. Jonah did not want the Ninevites to receive God's mercy. In the modern day church, who are the people who we believe are not worthy of God's mercy?

3. What are the implications of the two commandments (Mark 12:30-31)? How do they heal the Jonah Syndrome?

Chapter 4:

1. What is Missiopessimism? What does it look like in the Church?
2. According to the author, what is the problem with Missiopessimism?
3. What are the causes of Missiopessimism? Do you see these things at work in your own life?
4. How can we avoid falling prey to Missiopessimism? How can you apply the author's suggestions to your own life?

Chapter 5:

1. According to the author, what are the major reasons for church splitting among Diaspora churches?
2. How can churches, particularly church leaders, guard against a tendency to split?

Chapter 6:

1. The author maintains that the battle between Prioritism and Holism is a Western idea whereas Africans believe that sharing the Gospel and alleviating human suffering are inseparable. Do you agree? Why or why not?
2. How has Postmodernism made inroads into the Western Church?
3. How are Diaspora Christians uniquely suited to boldly preach the Gospel in the West? How can they use their experiences to embolden the Church and spread the Good News?

Chapter 7:

1. According to the author, what personal obstacles do Diaspora evangelists tend to face? Can you think of anymore?
2. Have you experienced one or more of these obstacles in your own life? How can you overcome these obstacles?

Chapter 8:

1. What are the two general dispositions the Diaspora Christians tend to fall into when it comes to their attitude in engaging Western culture?
2. Why are both attitudes dangerous?
3. Is there a balanced middle way?

Chapter 9:

1. What is ethnocentrism? How is it different from simply loving one's culture? Why is it so dangerous?
2. What are three causes of ethnocentrism, according to the author? Can you think of anymore?
3. What is the solution for ethnocentrism?

Chapter 10:

1. What is true about all of the people mentioned in Hebrews 11?
2. How can Diaspora believers live with the aim of "dying in faith" like their believing forefathers?

What is one way that you can apply what you have learned from this book in your life and in your church?

www.ingramcontent.com/pod-product-compliance
Lightning Source LLC
Chambersburg PA
CBHW072209090426
42740CB00012B/2449